The JOY *of* LOVE

GROUP READING GUIDE

to POPE FRANCIS' *Amoris Laetitia*

BILL HUEBSCH

TWENTY-THIRD
PUBLICATIONS
twentythirdpublications.com

ACKNOWLEDGMENTS

New Revised Standard Version Bible: Catholic Edition, copyright © 1989, 1993 the Division of Christian Education of the National Council of the Churches of Christ in the United States of America. Used by permission. All rights reserved.

Anything in quotation marks is an actual quote from the text of *Amoris Laetitia*.

TWENTY-THIRD PUBLICATIONS
1 Montauk Avenue, Suite 200, New London, CT 06320
(860) 437-3012 • (800) 321-0411 • www.23rdpublications.com

Cover photo: © Stefano Spaziani

ISBN: 978-1-62785-198-5
Printed in the U.S.A.

HOW TO USE THIS STUDY GUIDE
Six small group sessions

Participants are asked to read the introduction (articles 1–7) before the first session.

Gather. Welcome everyone to your group. Offer a special welcome to participants from other faith traditions who may join you. Ask participants to introduce themselves if needed.

As your class or group session gets underway, always begin with the Sign of the Cross. Pray Psalm 128 together, either in unison or in choir style. Ask God to bless your time together and send the Spirit to guide you.

Read. Moving around the circle in your group, read aloud the stanzas of this summary. Rotate readers with each paragraph. Group members should note items in the pope's teaching that strike them as especially important. Do not read aloud the article numbers. They are included to help you find this section in the original document if you want to explore in more depth certain elements of this apostolic exhortation.

Discuss and Pray. When you come to the group process notes, continue around the circle, discussing or praying as the notes direct. Use our suggestions as a starting point and add your own questions, prayers, or action plans.

Six sessions

SESSION ONE: *Chapters 1 Scriptural Reflections & 9 The Spirituality of Marriage*
SESSION TWO: *Chapters 2 Current Realities of Family & 3 The Vocation of Family*
SESSION THREE: *Chapter 4 Reflections on Love in Marriage*
SESSION FOUR: *Chapters 5 Welcoming Children & 7 Educating Children*
SESSION FIVE: *Chapter 6 Pastoral Perspectives on Marriage and Divorce*
SESSION SIX: *Chapter 8 Accompanying, Discerning, and Integrating Weakness in Marriage*

Finish. As you come to the end of your process, invite participants to identify the one or two large ideas that they hear the pope teaching in that day's segment of the document. Each participant may hear the text differently; there are no "correct" answers.

Conclude your session with a brief prayer and hospitality.

The JOY *of* LOVE

1 What we Christians proclaim about family life is good news! The Joy of Love that families experience is also the joy of the Church. **2**] Our bishops held two meetings to discuss the situation of families in today's world. Because the questions about family life are many and complex, more discussion is needed. Neither changing every rule nor applying all the rules with rigidity is sufficient to truly help families.

3 First of all, not all discussions about the doctrinal or moral aspects of family life need to be settled by the Church's central authority. We do need to have a unified teaching, but the Spirit will guide us to find pastoral approaches suited to each culture in every nation. Every general principle needs to be tailored to fit the cultural situation in which it is being lived, as we have long taught in the Church.

4 I am writing this apostolic exhortation in order to gather up the many contributions made by the world's bishops in the meetings mentioned above. I also want to add some other thoughts to help everyone reflect on this.

5 It's good to be writing this during our Jubilee of Mercy, because it is an invitation to families to value mercy in their households, and also because it encourages everyone to be a sign of mercy where it is most needed.

6 I'll first offer a Scriptural reflection in order to set a proper tone. I'll follow that with an examination of today's family life and a treatment of Church teaching on marriage. The two central chapters here will be concerned with love. I will then consider pastoral approaches that can help us, and I will offer a full chapter on raising children; I'll offer a frank discussion of situations in marriage that fall outside the norm, and I'll conclude with a brief discussion on family spirituality.

7 I don't recommend a hurried reading of this text. Read each chapter slowly and consider how it applies to your life. Married couples may benefit most from chapters four and five, pastoral ministers chapter six, and everyone chapter eight. Remember, "families are not a problem; they are first and foremost an opportunity."

Psalm 128

The Happy Home of the Faithful

✺

A Song of Ascents

Happy is everyone who fears the Lord,
who walks in his ways.

You shall eat the fruit of the labor of your hands;
you shall be happy, and it shall go well with you.

Your wife will be like a fruitful vine
within your house;

your children will be like olive shoots
around your table.

Thus shall the man be blessed
who fears the Lord.

The Lord bless you from Zion.

May you see the prosperity of Jerusalem
all the days of your life.

May you see your children's children.

Peace be upon Israel!

CHAPTER ONE

In the Light of the Word

8] The Bible is full of stories about families, stories about giving birth, loving deeply, and working through crises. Beginning with Adam and Eve in Genesis 1 and ending with the wedding feast of the Bride and the Lamb in Revelation 21, God speaks to us in Scripture as a family. Let us enter such a home now and allow Psalm 128 to lead us as we reflect on its meaning. (Prayerfully read Psalm 128.)

YOU AND YOUR WIFE [9–13]

9] At the center of the family are the father and mother, whose love story is the basis of life there. **10]** We were created for love, as the early chapters of Genesis teach us. We are created in God's image, male and female. The fruitfulness of the couple reflects the face of God. **11]** Such fruitful love is indeed a symbol of God's own inner life. Our ability to beget life is how the journey of salvation was carried forward. The community of the family is like the community of the Trinity, which is why St. Paul compared the union of Christ and the Church to a married couple.

12] Jesus reflected on the second chapter of Genesis when he taught in Matthew 19:5 about the bond in marriage as an intimate and solemn one, a direct encounter, the two becoming one flesh, as it were. The wonderful voice of the Song of Solomon puts it well: "My beloved is mine and I am his…I am my beloved's and my beloved is mine" (2:16; 6:3). **13**⟩ The marital union is thus a very close one, a clinging of one to the other, and a joining for life of bodies and souls. The hearts of the couple, joined with their children, form the family.

YOUR CHILDREN ARE AS THE SHOOTS OF AN OLIVE TREE [14–18]

14 Children enter a marriage as olive shoots growing on a healthy tree; they're full of energy and vitality. Throughout history, the presence of children has been a sign of the continuing family, generation after generation. **15**⟩ The household is actually a domestic church when our homes are filled with God's enduring presence and love. God thus blesses us. **16**⟩ The family is also that place where children are raised in the faith. Again, from generation to generation the faith is passed, one to the next, as parents become the first teachers of their children.

17 While parents have a serious responsibility to teach their children, the children for their part must honor and obey their parents. **18**⟩ Children also have their own lives to lead and must, at some point, part from their parents, while always continuing to honor them.

DISCUSSION
Share about your own experience of family. How did your family of origin become or fail to become a "domestic church"?

Does the pope's idyllic description of family here ring true in your experience?

A PATH OF SUFFERING AND BLOOD [19–22]

19 But this ideal family I am describing also fits into the real picture of family life, where there can be pain and violence. Families sometimes break up and fall apart. **20**⟩ This has been true from the beginning, as when Cain murdered his own brother. Down through history, family-based disputes have always been part of the story.

21 Jesus' own family was of modest means and had to flee as refugees to a foreign land. Throughout the gospels, Jesus hears about sick children, dying, divorce, anxiety, tension, and even violence. **22]** From all this we can clearly see that God does not instruct us with abstract ideas but rather accompanies us on our journeys. We hope in God's love, so that in time, "every tear shall be wiped away…" (Rev 21:4).

DISCUSSION

How have you experienced family challenges or even break-ups?

THE WORK OF YOUR HANDS [23–26]

23 Psalm 128 reminds us that work is an essential part of life. Our human dignity flows from the work of our hands. We were commissioned to "till and keep" the earth (Gen 2:15), and that is still our task. **24]** Such work, whether by the father or the mother, is also how the family is supported. **25]** It is for this reason that unemployment causes such suffering and takes a serious toll on family life.

26 Likewise, when people use nature abusively, ruining the earth and causing social imbalance, evil results.

THE TENDERNESS OF AN EMBRACE [27–30]

27 The principle given to us by Jesus for family life is self-giving love. "Such love bears fruit in mercy and forgiveness." **28]** In addition to family love is another virtue that is often overlooked: tenderness. Scripture provides this image and reminds us that God loves us with the same tenderness that exists between a mother and her child, tenderly held in her bosom.

29 Having and raising children thus reflects the life of the Trinity itself. God's creative work is accomplished in the family, which is why families are called to prayer, love, and life in the Church.

30 The Holy Family is our model. Daily life for them included burdens and nightmares; they fled the incredible violence of Herod, just like the many refugee families who flee violence today. Mary and Joseph faced their situation with courage; through them, we can also find meaning in family life.

DISCUSSION
*How do you see self-giving love (article 27) and tenderness
(article 28) playing a key role in the family?*

CHAPTER TWO

The Experiences and Challenges of Families

31 Because the welfare of the family is so important for the future of the world and the Church, I want to examine some of the family situations that the bishops addressed in their meetings and add to that my own concerns.

THE CURRENT REALITY OF THE FAMILY [32–49]

32 Families today experience greater freedom as the work of the household is shared more equitably. Old models of family life thus shift to newer models. **33**] Where such shifts in family life lead to extreme individualism or where each member of the family is an isolated unit, there is a danger. The drive to accumulate possessions and the fast pace of life both work against family peace. Freedom is a high value, but it can become self-centered if it is not used for the benefit of others.

34 Genuine freedom also entails commitment through thick and thin, in good times and in tough times. Our personal growth comes about, not by sweeping aside such commitments, but by embracing them as the means to growth.

35 Our Christian mission is to advocate for marriage as the way for women and men to respond to God's grace. It doesn't do much good to wring our hands and complain about present-day evils on one hand, or try to impose rigid authority on the other. Rather we should demonstrate the validity of our beliefs by living them authentically as a sign to the world.

36 "We need a healthy dose of self-criticism" to see that sometimes we have helped create the modern challenge to marriage by how we present our beliefs. Specifically, we have sometimes focused so much on procreation that we have ignored the value of the mutual love of the couple. We have also ignored modern concerns that young people have about the timing of families. And we have also spoken of marriage in too ideal a way, ignoring the reality of what really happens in daily life.

37 "We have long thought that simply by stressing doctrinal, bioethical and moral issues, without encouraging openness to grace, we were providing sufficient support to families, strengthening the marriage bond and giving meaning to marital life." We have found it hard to allow the consciences of the faithful to guide them. We in the Church are called to help form consciences, not replace them with our rules.

38 We are grateful for the many marriages in which love is central and family life holy. Many families do live their faith and pass it on to their children. But we have often wasted our pastoral energy by simply condemning life in today's world as evil without offering an alternate avenue to true happiness. Many people feel that the Church doesn't sound much like Jesus, who demanded an ideal from people but also was filled with mercy.

DISCUSSION
How has the Church either helped or hindered your growth as family, either in your family of origin or your current situation?

39 This doesn't mean we should ever stop speaking up for self-giving love and pointing out where it is lacking. We must point out that relationships don't start and stop in real life like they do in social media. We do tend to treat each other as "disposable" sometimes, just as we do material goods, food, and even the environment. But we know that everything is circular: those who use or abuse others will eventually be used and abused themselves, all in a dark circle of despair.

40 Thus young people today often postpone a wedding or having children either because they fear there is no future for them or because they want to first build up their wealth. Marriage is thus devalued. People fear they will lose their freedom by making a commitment, but we need to demonstrate that the opposite is actually true. Commitments make us free to love.

41 The lack of self-giving love leads to a sort of narcissism based on being unilateral in one's life rather than relational. This naturally leads then to a culture where pornography, prostitution, casual use of sex, and commercialization of the body emerge. People begin acting only in their own self-interest, and martial problems result. Marriage is about working together in love, but when couples give up on working things out and seek instead new partners, we see a serious breakdown of family. **42**] Likewise, the trend to having fewer children—for whatever reasons—leads to a loss of hope in the future.

43 The decline in some areas of participation in the life of the Church also adds to this, because families feel more isolated because of it. Governments also focus on individuals over families, leading to difficulty in raising children, seeing the old as a burden, and outbreaks of violence.

44 A lack of affordable housing in some places also adds to this challenge. Likewise, the lack of adequate and affordable health care contributes to the challenges families face, as does the lack of educational opportunities. And finally, when families must separate in order to find sufficient work, they cannot grow together as they should.

45 This litany goes on: children born outside marriage, sexual exploitation of children, societies enduring violence and war, terrorism and organized crime, and

14

homelessness—all eat away at family life. **46**] Forced migration likewise hurts family life, both for those who migrate as well as for those who remain behind. This is especially true for women and children. **47**] Families who are raising children with disabilities or special needs also face special challenges and demonstrate God's great love by their efforts. We must support them.

48 Care for the elderly is also a challenge to families today. It often puts a financial or emotional strain on the household, especially when the needs of the older persons are great. In order to work against euthanasia, we must assist families to care for their aged members. **49**] Finally, the problems faced by poor households, especially where single mothers must also work outside the home, are also our concern here. We should not judge them but assist them in their needs.

DISCUSSION

Which of the pope's points here do you find more
present in your own family or community?

SOME CHALLENGES [50–57]

50 Daily life in the home is important, and when spouses return from a day's work exhausted, not wanting to interact with the children, and often not sharing a meal, a breakdown occurs. Families may watch too much TV or use the Internet more than they talk to each other. Or they may be so intent on growing financially comfortable that they neglect the present moment. **51**] Drug use, alcoholism, and other addictions add to this breakdown, as do violence and abuse. This leads ultimately to higher levels of violence on the streets.

52 The weakening of the family hurts society as a whole. There are a variety of family situations that do offer stability today, but we must also say that temporary or same-sex unions may not be simply equated with marriage.

53 Other challenges to marriage include polygamy, arranged marriages, and living together before marriage. We don't want to maintain the old model of marriage marked by authoritarianism and violence, but we do argue for marriages that offer exclusivity, permanence, and openness to life. As the bishops said in the report after their 2015 meeting on the family, "The strength of the family lies in its capacity to love and to teach how to love. For all a family's problems, it can always grow, beginning with love."

54 I also want to mention the shameful ways in which women are treated in certain places. It is wrong for them to be subjected to violence, verbal and physical abuse, mutilation, and enslavement. Men and women share equal dignity, and we want to see all forms of discrimination against women eliminated. **55**] We urge fathers to be present—not absent—in family life. Such absence can be physical, emotional, or spiritual.

56 We also see today a trend that sees no difference between male and female genders, but we believe there is a distinct biological difference between men and women and that it is implanted within us by the Creator.

57 Many families know they are far from perfect, and yet they live in true love. There is no stereotype of a "perfect family" that we can describe, but daily life in the household continues to be a journey of many realities. We don't want to fall into "doleful laments" about the challenges before us but seek new ways to help people find hope and truth.

DISCUSSION

In your particular community, what are the most important challenges to marriage?

What is your personal experience of these challenges?

CHAPTER THREE

Looking to Jesus: The Vocation of the Family

58 In the family, the "kerygma" must resound. This means that the family members should remind one another constantly that "God loves us; Jesus offers us his self-giving love on the cross; he now walks with us in the Spirit in our daily lives; and we are also called to walk with one another in love."

59 What we teach about marriage and family life must be inspired by the tenderness and love of this message or it will become nothing more than a dry and lifeless body of doctrine. **60]** This brief chapter will summarize what we teach about marriage, starting with the tender gaze with which Jesus looks upon us all. He gazed with the same tenderness on the men and women whom he met with love. We might speak of this as "the gospel of the family."

JESUS RESTORES AND FULFILS GOD'S PLAN [61–66]

61 Our first principle is that marriage is a gift from God, including sexuality. **62]** The second principle flows from the first, and it is that marriage, once entered into freely, is indissoluble. **63]** The spouses find their ultimate meaning in the covenant into which they enter. Grace is present to assist the couple in building a loving marriage. Thus the gospel of the family spans the history of the world.

64 Jesus' encounters with marriage throughout his ministry support this. He demonstrated the true meaning of mercy as he sympathized with grieving parents, welcomed the woman at the well in Samaria, and forgave the woman who wept at his feet. **65]** The very birth of Jesus, when we contemplate its meaning, fills us with hope and joy. **66]** Just as Mary and Joseph created a home, so our homes also become a light in the darkness of the world.

THE FAMILY IN THE DOCUMENTS OF THE CHURCH [67–70]

67 In the *Constitution on the Church in the Modern World* article 48, Vatican II defined marriage as a community of life and love. It extolled the place of self-giving love and sexual loving (article 49). And it declared again that Christ is present in every marriage. **68]** In *Humanae Vitae,* Blessed Paul VI highlighted the connection between sexual lovemaking and the creation of a new life, calling couples to responsible parenthood (article 10).

69 St. John Paul II wrote a letter to families in which he outlined the vocation of men and women and provided guidelines for the pastoral care of the family. Sexual love, he said, leads to deeper mutual love and is part of the call to holiness (*Familiaris Consortio* article 13). **70]** Pope Benedict XVI likewise extolled the place of love in marriage and connected that to the role of self-giving love, as Christ demonstrated on the cross.

DISCUSSION

In your own words, how is marriage a reflection of the
good news that Jesus loves us, gave himself up for us, and
now walks with us every day (the kerygma)?

18

THE SACRAMENT OF MATRIMONY [71–75]

71 Jesus raised marriage to the level of a sacrament, and through it couples receive the grace of the Holy Spirit to build and sustain true love. **72**] This sacrament is a gift that enriches the couple. It also reminds the Church of what happened on the cross. Marriage is a vocation, and the sacrament is a public celebration of that.

73 I say again: mutual self-giving love is the ground of this sacrament. Such self-giving begins in baptism and is sustained in the Eucharist. The sacrament is not a mere social convention but the very heart of the Church. It is a sign of how much Christ loves us. **74**] Sexual lovemaking is made holy by the sacrament and leads to grace in the life of the couple. Their common household life likewise flows from the sacrament. In it, the couple responds to their vocation.

75 In the Latin tradition, the man and woman are the ministers of the sacrament. Their consent and their sexual union are the outward signs of the sacrament. God acts in the rite; and in the Oriental Churches this is made clear through the blessing that the couple receives.

SEEDS OF THE WORD AND IMPERFECT SITUATIONS [76–79]

76 The gospel of the family also includes seeds of faith that are waiting to grow. There is mystery in marriage, and the couple may not understand immediately all the gifts that God offers them through it. **77**] "Natural marriage" is by its nature sacramental when entered into by baptized people. Any family that shows the Spirit alive and at work within it, leading to mutual love, openness to children, fidelity, and permanence, will receive our appreciation.

78 To those who are living together, married civilly, or divorced and remarried, the Church also extends its pastoral care. We encourage them to do good, take loving care of each other, and serve their communities.

79 Pastors should always exercise careful discernment in working with such families. "The degree of responsibility" for the situation may not be equal, or "factors may exist which limit the ability to make a decision." Pastors should avoid judgments; they should take into account the complexity of people's situations.

DISCUSSION

How can pastors and pastoral leaders best accompany married couples on their journey through life? What pastoral care should the Church offer?

THE TRANSMISSION OF LIFE AND THE REARING OF CHILDREN [80–85]

80 "Marriage is firstly an 'intimate partnership of life and love'" (*Church in the Modern World* article 48) "which is a good for the spouses themselves" (Canon Law article 1055) "while sexuality 'is ordered to the conjugal love of man and woman'" (*Catechism of the Catholic Church* article 2360). However, "spouses to whom God has not granted children can have a conjugal life full of meaning, in both human and Christian terms" (*Catechism* article 1654). Every act of sexual love must embrace this meaning even if, for various reasons, no conception results.

81 Children are a gift, and they flow from sexual lovemaking because God created it to be so. **82]** Children are not one element in a couple's "life plan" but are integral to the couple's married life. Adoption and foster parenting also express this same fruitfulness.

83 Because life is so sacred, there cannot be an argument made for the rights of the mother to manage her body without also arguing for the rights of the child within her to be born. Children are not property. In the same vein, we urgently assert the right to a natural death, and we reject the death penalty as anti-life.

84 The Church has a role to play in educating children, but the primary responsibility for this remains with the parents. Schools or religious education programs do not replace parents but support and enforce what parents do. **85]** The Church is called to help parents fulfill their role but not to replace them with a program.

THE FAMILY AND THE CHURCH [86–88]

86 We encourage those families working to make their household into a domestic church, one in which work, love, forgiveness, and reflection are part and parcel of daily life. **87**] The Church is indeed a family of families, gathering to support and sustain each other. Safeguarding the family is essential for the Church. **88**] Family love is beautiful; it is the purpose of marriage. Families celebrate their happiness together and walk together through more difficult times.

DISCUSSION

What are the purposes of marriage, in your own words?

How can we teach others how to welcome children generously?

What does your parish do to support family life?

CHAPTER FOUR

Love in Marriage

89 Now we must speak about *love* because love is the basis of marriage. In our day and age, the word *love* is often misunderstood; so let us study it together for our mutual benefit.

OUR DAILY LOVE [90]

90 Let us meditate on this wonderful passage of Scripture: "Love is patient; love is kind; love is not envious or boastful or arrogant or rude. It does not insist on its own way; it is not irritable or resentful; it does not rejoice in wrongdoing, but rejoices in the truth. It bears all things, believes all things, hopes all things, endures all things" (1 Cor 13:4–7).

LOVE IS PATIENT [91–92]

91 The biblical meaning of this phrase entails understanding how God is merciful to us. In the life of our family, we too must imitate God, whose mercy endures forever. **92]** Being patient does not mean allowing others to mistreat us! If we think that the world and all people should be perfect, or if we make ourselves the constant center of our attention, then when things are not as we think they should be we react with aggression. We become angry. But on the other hand, we become patient when we put aside bitterness, judgment, and anger. Then we realize that others have a right to be who they are. Even if we're annoyed a little, love leads us to be patient.

LOVE IS AT THE SERVICE OF OTHERS [93-94]

93 Beyond being patient we are also called to *act*! Love leads us to help others. We call this readiness to be of assistance *being kind*. **94]** Love is more than a feeling. It is a set of decisions that we take to put others first. This leads us to the happiness of giving and spending ourselves on behalf of others without asking to be repaid.

LOVE IS NOT JEALOUS [95-96]

95 Love leads us to rejoice in the good fortune of others, not be unhappy about it. If we are sad because of someone else's success, it shows we are more concerned about ourselves than them. Love moves us to rise above our own world to value the achievements of others. This is so freeing!

96 In this way, love leads us to embrace the commandments not to covet or desire what belongs to another. But it goes further by calling us to a sincere and profound esteem for others. You say to yourself that you love this person, so you see him or her with the eyes of God, whose generosity is boundless. Likewise, we reject injustice, especially when some have more than they need while others suffer with too little.

LOVE IS NOT BOASTFUL [97–98]

97 Love leads us to focus on others rather than ourselves, and we do this by avoiding haughty bragging or pushy behavior. We refrain from speaking about ourselves all the time and focus the attention on others. This all means that love leads us to avoid becoming too "puffed up" with our own accomplishments, because we know all we have is a gift. What really makes us important is to love with understanding and to embrace the weak.

98 When supposedly mature people of faith start thinking they know more than anyone else, a form of boasting is underway. Love is marked by humility. Loving others means understanding, forgiving, and serving, not lording it over. Remember 1 Peter 5:5? "And all of you must clothe yourselves with humility…"

LOVE IS NOT RUDE [99–100]

99 Love is not harsh, but it is gentle and careful with others and their feelings. It does not lead us to be abrasive, because love leads us to avoid making others suffer anything at all. We therefore live agreeably with each other, with sensitivity, tenderness, and empathy.

100 Rather than readily pointing out people's shortcomings, love leads us to see the good and to look kindly upon each other. Everything we have said so far about love comes into play here: being patient, rejoicing in others' success, and keeping our focus on the good of the beloved. We speak words of comfort, consolation, and encouragement. Jesus spoke like this to people, and we must learn to imitate Jesus' own gentleness with each other.

DISCUSSION
Tell stories from your own experience that reflect this teaching.
When and with whom did you experience this or fail to experience it?

LOVE IS GENEROUS [101–102]

101 We look in love to the interests of others rather than to our own. This makes us generous, and our generosity is natural to us. It's more important in the reign of

God to serve than to be served. **102**] So our desire then is to desire to become more loving, not to desire that we would be more loved, as St. Thomas Aquinas pointed out. Love expects nothing in return, even if what we are called to give is our own very life.

LOVE IS NOT IRRITABLE OR RESENTFUL [103–104]

103 Resentment eats away at our souls, leaving us unhappy and irritated with others. When we are indignant toward others, we only hurt our own selves. **104**] Love leads us to avoid nurturing anger and resentment toward others. We may feel an urge of hostility, but grace empowers us to refuse to be dominated by it. We should not go to bed at night with anger in our hearts. Instead, let us make peace in our homes through small gestures, just enough to communicate our love for our family.

DISCUSSION

Tell stories from your own experience that reflect this teaching.
When and with whom did you experience this or fail to experience it?

LOVE FORGIVES [105–108]

105 Here is the key to love: forgive constantly and fully. We try to understand other people's weaknesses and limitations without judging them. We stop looking for faults in others. We don't assume that every mistake is an intentionally done offense against us. We focus instead on others instead of ourselves and turn our desire for vengeance into love.

106 Forgiveness is not easy but, with practice, it becomes more and more possible for us. Family harmony can only be achieved when forgiveness is a theme. **107**] Forgiving others, we know, also means forgiving ourselves. If others criticize us, we may feel less than acceptable. But if we pray over our past history, lean into our limitations, and yes, even laugh at and forgive our own foibles, we will have the same attitude toward others.

108 We can do this because we experience God forgiving us first. God's love for us transcends everything we do, because God loves us while we continue to offend and sin. Our family life will be filled with tension and mutual criticism unless we ourselves imitate God by unconditional love and forgiveness of each other.

DISCUSSION

Tell stories from your own experience that reflect this teaching. When and with whom did you experience this or fail to experience it?

LOVE REJOICES WITH OTHERS [109–110]

109 If we rejoice when others suffer or have injustice done to them, then we are far away from understanding love. Love calls us to rejoice in what is good and only in that. We value the dignity and talents of others without comparing or competing with them. We certainly never secretly rejoice in their failings. **110**] Instead, we try to do good to others and to make sure their happiness is paramount in our outlook. Love calls us to be happy for the happiness of others, and to celebrate that within the family is wonderful!

LOVE BEARS ALL THINGS [111-113]

111 Love empowered by God in this way can survive any threat. **112**] In simple English, this means that we sometimes have to hold our tongues. We limit how we judge others and control that impulse to be ruthless in condemning them. Rather than letting fly with a litany of judgments that reduce our opponent to rubble, we hold our tongue and do not speak against each other with anger. We bear all things patiently; this is a very specific requirement of God's law.

113 In marriage, couples speak well of each other. They try to show each other's good side, not each other's faults. And this isn't done only when in front of those outside the family, but it is an interior state of mind, a holding the other in high esteem and simply looking the other way regarding small faults. We learn that we need not be perfect in order to be loved, which is also how God loves us. In marriage each partner loves the other the best they can, imperfections and all.

DISCUSSION

Tell stories from your own experience that reflect this teaching.
When and with whom did you experience this or fail to experience it?

LOVE BELIEVES ALL THINGS [114–115]

114 When we speak of believing all things, we don't mean the same thing as when we speak of faith. Here the meaning leads to trust. In marriage we come to believe in each other. **115**] Such trust allows us to be free. We need not control each other, possess each other, or dominate each other. We share with one another as spouses, and at the same time, we are free to be transparent with each other. This removes the need for suspicion, secrets, and hiding our faults.

LOVE HOPES ALL THINGS [116–117]

116 Hope is possible in marriage when the partners believe together in the future. We mature together, grow old together, always hoping in one another. Not everything will turn out as we wish, but God works good out of whatever occurs. **117**] For we hope that, after death, we will be joined together for eternity. Then every tear will indeed be wiped away, every fault and failure forgiven, and our true person will shine forth.

LOVE ENDURES ALL THINGS [118–119]

118 Love gives marriage endurance. This allows us to bear with certain aggravations, but also to look beyond them. This is love that *never gives up,* no matter what. Martin Luther King helps us understand this. He believed that people who hated him most still had some good in them. He saw the image of God in everyone, which taught him how to love his enemy: "when the opportunity presents itself for you to defeat your enemy, that is the time which you must not do it," he said.

119 In family life we want to grow in that sort of love that helps us resist every evil that might threaten it. Here again is the love that never gives up. Even when a couple has separated because of serious incompatibility, still the partners continue to help each other when needed.

DISCUSSION

Tell stories from your own experience that reflect this teaching.
When and with whom did you experience this or fail to experience it?

GROWING IN CONJUGAL LOVE [120–122]

120 Erotic, sexual love is made possible by all that we have said here so far. When it occurs in the context of love that is patient, kind, and forgiving, it is infused by the Holy Spirit and leads the couple to ever deeper love. **121**] This love leads the couple in marriage to a deep and profound bond, one that mirrors the way in which God loves us. It is love in the image of God. **122**] This doesn't mean that the partners in marriage are perfect or need to be. It only means they are growing constantly in how much they love each other.

LIFELONG SHARING [123–125]

123 Sexual loving is a great form of friendship—the greatest form! It expresses concern for the good of the other, intimacy, warmth, comfort, stability, and a shared life. The couple is sharing their whole lives; "lovers do not see their relationship as merely temporary." All of this is rooted in what it means to be human; it is inborn.

124 Love that is weak and incapable of marriage cannot sustain such a great, lifelong commitment. It is ephemeral and does not stand the test of time. Only with grace is such a long-lasting love possible. It is, as our faith teaches us, a great mystery how such love is even possible.

125 So marriage is passionate, but it is also friendship. Marriage is not intended only to produce children but also to support the mutual love of the couple. As the *Constitution on the Church in the Modern World* from Vatican II puts it in article 50, "such a love, bringing together the human and the divine, leads the partners to a free and mutual self-giving, experienced in tenderness and action, and permeating their entire lives."

DISCUSSION

Tell stories from your own experience that reflect this teaching.
When and with whom did you experience this or fail to experience it?

JOY AND BEAUTY [126–130]

126 In order to cultivate joy in marriage, we must see that such joy can exist even in the midst of great sorrow. We accept that marriage is a mix of struggles, tensions, pain, satisfaction, pleasures, annoyances, and longings. Joy comes in the midst of all that marriage offers us.

127 In marriage the partners hold each other in high esteem out of love and charity for each other. We see the sacredness of the other; we see their beauty, not in the way that the society sees beauty but in the way that a true lover beholds his or her beloved one. We give each other tenderness, freedom, and immense respect. We marvel at their goodness.

128 Even as we grow old and infirm, our partners continue to see us as beautiful. We gaze on one another with appreciation; how very sad when we withhold this from each other. Love opens our eyes to see our beloved as a human being of great worth.

129 We want to cultivate our ability to offer each other such affirmation, for in it there is also great joy. We want to bring delight to our spouse; this is not the work of a vain or self-centered person but that of a lover who wants only good for his or her beloved. **130**] Even when there is pain and sorrow in life, such joy is possible. Couples know that it is worth it to struggle and suffer together. They have grown as a couple. There is no greater joy than to achieve something significant with the one you love.

DISCUSSION

Tell stories from your own experience that reflect this teaching.
When and with whom did you experience this or fail to experience it?

MARRYING FOR LOVE [131–132]

131 Let me say to young people that no love is lost when you marry. Rather, choosing marriage as a public statement of your commitment enhances the love. This is much stronger than a temporary arrangement for your mutual gratification; it is love with a purpose, love that lasts, love that is lifelong and strong.

132 To choose marriage is to join your pathways in life and walk together, come what may. This is not something to enter into carelessly, because such a commitment always involves some risk. It you are truly in love, though, then marriage is the way you demonstrate that to each other and to the world. The "yes" you give in marriage echoes throughout the years of your life.

A LOVE THAT REVEALS ITSELF AND INCREASES [133–135]

133 In order for love to become real, it must enter into our daily lives and not sit on the sidelines. In the family, three words are needed, as I have said before, and they are "Please," "Thanks," and "Sorry." Do not be stingy about using these words with each other, because they protect your love.

134 The love that exists on the day of the wedding is not enough. Love must grow throughout the marriage, grow constantly larger and more generous. Marriage doesn't present you with a "duty" to stay together but with the grace to grow in love.

Specific acts of kindness, acts of love and affirmation, gifts, and sweet words—these are what make love grow.

135 In short, we should always remember that "the best is yet to come" in marriage and love. Families are real; people get sick, grow old, become forgetful, and are not as beautiful as on the day of the wedding, but it is all good.

DISCUSSION

Tell stories from your own experience that reflect this teaching.
When and with whom did you experience this or fail to experience it?

DIALOGUE [136–141]

136 The partners in marriage learn to talk with each other and express their inner thoughts and feelings. Silence is a killer in marriage. We learn over time how to dialogue well, how to use a proper tone, how to time our remarks, and how to communicate well.

137 This all requires that the couple has time together—alone and undisturbed— and often. We need not offer each other every opinion we have but rather to be sure we have heard what the other has to say. This requires an interior silence so that we become good listeners. You can't rush this. We normally don't need our partner to solve the problem we face but only to hear what we are trying to say.

138 Do not downplay what your partner tells you, but hold it in high esteem. Give real importance to their feelings and experiences of life. Put yourself in their shoes and acknowledge each other's truths.

139 In order for such love to progress, you must keep an open mind and be careful not to let your own opinions and ideas bog you down. When you bring the thoughts of both of you together, a new idea emerges better than either of the old. We need to be able to speak without fear that we will offend one another, and this means speaking with measured words, kind words, and sincere words. Don't let anger or hurt rule your conversation.

140 Such sincere and honest conversation is easier when you show affection for one another. Love overcomes all other barriers. **141**] Finally, it is necessary for each partner in marriage to have a rich reflection and prayer life, for out of such quiet centeredness arises the profound truths that we share with each other.

> ### DISCUSSION
> *Tell stories from your own experience that reflect this teaching.*
> *When and with whom did you experience this or fail to experience it?*

PASSIONATE LOVE [142]
142 Sexual love must have within it both pleasure and passion in order to adequately reflect the union of the human heart with God. Let us speak now about feelings and sexuality in marriage.

THE WORLD OF EMOTIONS [143–146]
143 Feelings are part and parcel of married life. We awaken them in each other, and they play a vital role. **144**] Jesus showed his emotions throughout his ministry. **145**] The experience of an emotion is morally neutral; everyone has emotions. But how we allow these emotions to drive us is under our own control. Likewise, the desire to love isn't itself the same as love. One may be caught up in selfish desires that render him or her incapable for true self-giving love. **146**] Family life is enriched when the emotions that drive it are healthy and at the service of the family.

GOD LOVES THE JOY OF HIS CHILDREN [147–149]
147 The Church embraces erotic sexual activity when it is honest and loving. **148**] Sexual activity is honest and loving when it is in balance with generous commit-

ment, patient hope, and the willingness to struggle toward an ideal in the family. **149**] God is pleased when we enjoy our world—bodies, souls, hearts, and all. As couples grow and mature, their pleasures do as well.

THE EROTIC DIMENSION OF LOVE [150–152]

150 God created sex, and it is a marvelous gift he has given us. If we teach that it should be cultivated carefully, it is only to prevent it from becoming inauthentic. **151**] This doesn't mean there cannot be spontaneity in sexual loving. On the contrary, as love matures, a sense of wonder and surprise grows with it. Through sex, the couple experiences their most real and true selves—and this is a great gift from God.

152 So sex is much more than a permissible evil in marriage. Rather, we see it as a gift from God that enriches the relationship of the couple. When it is freely and joyfully shared, we can truly feel that "life has turned out good and happy."

DISCUSSION

Tell stories from your own experience that reflect this teaching.
When and with whom did you experience this or fail to experience it?

VIOLENCE AND MANIPULATION [153–157]

153 We do know, however, that in our modern culture, sex can become depersonalized and unhealthy, and we must guard against that. We cannot view our married partner as good only as long as he or she is young and strong; we must be willing to grow old together. **154**] Within marriage, sex can become manipulative, coercive, or violent. It cannot be imposed on our partner without his or her willing it.

155 We must likewise avoid turning sex into a habit of which we cannot get enough. Couples need space between them, emotional and physical. Each partner brings her or his own dignity to the sexual love. If there is domination, that dignity is lost.

156 Any time sex involves submission, we reject it. In the Letter to the Ephesians, it is true that Paul tells women to "be subject to your husbands," but this passage reflects a cultural reality of the first century that no longer exists today. In marriage, neither partner can be a slave to the other. This text is often misread; in truth, the text and the verses following it are meant to call everyone to be subject *to one another*, to take each other into account fully.

157 But while we reject distortions of sex, we do not reject sex itself. In marriage it is not enough for one partner to always give him or herself to the other; it is also necessary to receive love, as Pope Benedict has taught. We are fragile people, and we must take great care to shepherd our sexual lives toward love and fidelity.

DISCUSSION

Tell stories from your own experience that reflect this teaching.
When and with whom did you experience this or fail to experience it?

MARRIAGE AND VIRGINITY [158–162]

158 Many people who are not married are devoted to family as well. They also serve the wider community and often consecrate their lives to this service. **159]** "Virginity is a form of love." It allows one to focus the heart on the things of God. St. Paul recognized this and chose virginity for himself. Marriage is not inferior to virginity, nor is celibacy superior to marriage. They are of equal value to the life of the Church. **160]** Perfection in the spiritual life can be achieved by people in either state.

161 Virginity and marital love both reflect the kingdom of God, although in different ways. The former is a sign of the freedom of the kingdom while the latter reflects the love of the Trinity. **162]** Celibacy can become nothing more than a comfortable single life that provides freedom to be independent. Married love can be a witness of selflessness and generosity. Parents care for their children. Spouses care for each other as they grow old or incapacitated.

DISCUSSION

Tell stories from your own experience that reflect this teaching.

When and with whom did you experience this or fail to experience it?

THE TRANSFORMATION OF LOVE [163–164]

163 When the sexual urge declines, the intimacy of the marriage does not. Couples can remain companions on life's journey "until death do them part." Love goes beyond emotions; it is a lifelong decision to be there for the other, and couples recommit to this daily as they share meals, projects, dreams, and visions. **164]** In the final years of life, the marriage bond remains strong and finds a new form of expression besides that of sexual loving.

DISCUSSION

Tell stories from your own experience that reflect this teaching.

When and with whom did you experience this or fail to experience it?

In what ways do celibacy and virginity contribute to love?

CHAPTER FIVE

Love Made Fruitful

165 Love always gives life, and for the married couple that life is often a new child, a permanent sign of their unity and love.

WELCOMING A NEW LIFE [166–167]

166 In the family, new life is welcomed as a gift. What a symbol of God's love, for babies are loved before they're even born! And yet many children are unwanted, abandoned, and robbed of their childhood. We must do all we can to change this, for the first act of the parents is to accept the gift of the new child, entrusted to the mother and father, and to guide the child to human fulfillment.

167 Large families are a joy, but parents should not engage in unlimited procreation, because raising children requires common sense, proper finances, and the right social setting.

LOVE AND PREGNANCY [168–171]

168 "Pregnancy is a difficult but wonderful time." Each woman shares in the mystery of creation and is part of the plan of God. Each child has a place in God's heart from the moment of conception onward. **169]** Every mother and father dream about the child, and those dreams prepare them for family life.

170 The entire code of life is written in the genetic code in the embryonic stage of life, yet only God fully knows this child at this stage. If the parents do not want this child, we urge them to ask for the strength and courage to accept it; every child must feel wanted. We love children for being children, not for being convenient, correct, or the right gender. **171**] I urge mothers to feel a serene excitement as they await the birth of their child.

THE LOVE OF A MOTHER AND A FATHER [172–177]

172 Once born, the love continues. The child is named, given a language, looked upon with love, and the dreams continue. Each of the spouses contributes to the raising of the child. The mutual love of the couple transfers to the child.

173 We recognize, of course, that women wish to study, work, and pursue personal goals, but this must be in balance with the need of the child for the mother to be present, especially in the early years. Feminism must include motherhood as one of its features. **174**] The mother's love is the strongest antidote to selfishness and individualism, for they teach love by loving. Their tender assurance to the child is essential. "Dear mothers: thank you! Thank you for what you are in your family and for what you give to the Church and the world."

175 The mother offers the child tenderness and compassion, helping him or her to feel welcome and to grow in self-esteem. The father helps the child be open to the challenges life will offer, helping prepare the child for hard work. Both roles are essential. **176**] In some cultures the fathers tend to be absent from the family dynamic, and this opens up a gap in the balance of life. While a return to authoritarianism is not needed, households do need good order for the sake of the children. **177**] The father must always be present in the family, without becoming controlling. Children need the stability of a father to whom they can turn when needed.

DISCUSSION

What elements of the pope's teaching here touch your heart most directly?

What challenges you in this teaching?

What affirms the decisions and pathways of your life?

AN EXPANDING FRUITFULNESS [178–184]

178 We know that not all couples are able to have children, but this does not diminish the value of their marriage. **179**] Adoption is a generous act and provides a child with a home. Legislation should make adoption possible without complicating it.

180 Children are persons in their own right, and the best interests of the child should come into play when decisions about adoption and foster care are being made. Trafficking of children between nations, however, should be prevented. **181**] Having children is not the only way for a family to be fruitful. The household can become a hub for integrating people into society.

182 Families should not see themselves as overly different or set apart from others. Being an average family, raising children, and providing care for neighbors is sufficient. **183**] The family is a place where outcasts are welcomed and the fight for justice is staged, and the family shares its life with others. Such families find a place for the poor, build friendships with the less fortunate, and treat everyone as "other Christs." **184**] By how they live as well as by what they say in words, families echo Jesus to the world.

DISCERNING THE BODY [185–186]

185 We must mention here that wealthy families should not shun poor ones, especially at the Eucharist. **186**] There should not be divisions or distinctions among us when we gather for Mass. The Mass calls on us as families to open our doors to greater fellowship with the less privileged. Receiving Eucharist is at the same time receiving the poor and suffering into our hearts and homes.

LIFE IN THE WIDER FAMILY [187]

187 The wider family—aunts, uncles, grandparents, cousins—is important for the raising of the children. It provides them with a large nest and prevents a sense of isolation for everyone.

BEING SONS AND DAUGHTERS [188–190]

188 "We are all sons and daughters." We did not give ourselves life, so we should always remember our parents. **189]** The fourth commandments teaches us to honor our parents, and this is important for a truly humane society. **190]** But while parents should not be abandoned, the man and woman who marry do need to leave them so that the new home will be a true hearth and the couple can grow as "one flesh." One's parents should not be confidential to all the secrets of married life.

THE ELDERLY [191–193]

191 We must reawaken the sense of gratitude and appreciation for the older members of our families. Do not "throw them away," but treasure and honor them always. **192]** The elderly help us appreciate the continuity of generations. They are sources of wisdom, and their presence offers children even more stability. **193]** Listening to the elderly tell their stories from life provides a bridge to the past and a window to the future. Children need to sink their roots in the rich soil of a collective history.

BEING BROTHERS AND SISTERS [194–195]

194 The relationship of brothers and sisters is the basis of all society. **195**] Growing up with sisters and brothers provides a school of care, patience, and affection. When there is only one child, steps should be taken to socialize that child among others.

A BIG HEART [196–198]

196 Beyond the couple and their children is also the larger family, which includes friends, neighbors, and even hangers-on. **197**] This larger family provides support, love, and counsel to the parents. It includes young people in their struggles, the unmarried, separated, widowed, and alone. Even those who have made a mess of their lives are included. **198**] And, of course, the larger family also includes the in-laws! The culture and customs of both family systems should come into the life of the couple, and it is all part of family life.

DISCUSSION

What elements of the pope's teaching here touch your heart most directly?

What challenges you in this teaching?

What affirms the decisions and pathways of your life?

CHAPTER SIX

Some Pastoral Perspectives

199 I now wish to provide a reflection on some significant pastoral challenges we face in today's families and marriages.

PROCLAIMING THE GOSPEL OF THE FAMILY TODAY [200–204]

200 It is important that people experience the gospel of the family as a true joy in their lives. We wish to reach out to families with humility and mercy, not showing some impersonal generic concern for "the idea of family" but actually touching real situations. **201**] Pastoral care for families must reach into the deepest longings of the heart, the desire for belonging, community, and fruitfulness. In this outreach, presenting rules is not enough; we must also encourage the values needed for families to prosper.

202 The parish is the main place where such pastoral outreach will occur. The parish is a family of families, after all. The formation of the clergy and other ministers must be realistic to help them deal with the complexities of modern life. **203**] Seminarians should be formed beyond doctrine to understand and appreciate family life. Families, lay people, and especially women should, in fact, be part of seminary training since the field of ministry for the priest will be family life. **204**] We also need lay leaders to assist in the pastoral care of families, including the many professional family social workers, medical personnel, counselors, and others.

DISCUSSION

How can we best reach out to families with mercy today?

PREPARING ENGAGED COUPLES FOR MARRIAGE [205–211]

205 We want to help young people discover the beauty and dignity of marriage. **206**] We want to help the engaged couple to ground their marriage in the life of the parish and to benefit from learning the values of the Christian community.

207 The community itself benefits from the journey of the engaged couple, but we must set their preparation in the midst of the community, not alongside or outside it. Each local Church should decide how to best prepare couples for marriage. Marriage preparation is not the time to teach the whole of Christian doctrine; rather, let us encourage and prepare the couple for a lifetime of faith.

208 The goal of the preparation is to help the couple learn how to love the very real person with whom they plan to spend the rest of their lives; so while general courses and talks are helpful, there is also the need for individual discussion. The best teacher will be the couple's own parents, giving witness to their own Christian lives.

209 We all know that marriage also involves challenges and risks, and the preparation process should take this into account. If the couple is not compatible, now is the time to realize that, especially if they have not previously discussed matters on which they may disagree. Hence the importance of individual couple preparation. **210**] Couples need help to detect danger signals in their relationship before the wedding. We don't want couples to marry who do not know each other at this deep and profound level.

211 Weddings do not create marriages! The marriage of the couple emerges slowly as they grow in love, faith, and understanding of each other. The wedding celebrates a reality that is already present—that the hearts of the couple have become one. We need for this a "pedagogy of love" attuned to the feelings and needs of the couple. They should make use of the sacrament of reconciliation to bring their past sins and mistakes to healing and resolution.

THE PREPARATION OF THE CELEBRATION [212–216]

212 Preparation for the wedding is different from preparation for marriage. Attention to the details of the celebration, such as invitations, menus, and clothing, are important, but they should not overtake the rest. Some couples defer marriage because they can't afford the wedding, but let me say: be courageous and be different. Opt for a simpler event and make marriage your priority.

213 We want the couple to make personal the liturgical celebration and to understand each of the signs. Their free consent and their sexual union are the outward signs of this sacrament and should be seen as central. **214]** The words of consent should be taken seriously because they shed light on everything else in the ceremony. **215]** This is about more than a mere wedding; it's about a lifetime of faithful marriage that will involve children, in-laws, challenges, sacrifices, and work. The language of sexual loving becomes a key part of their lives.

216 Marriage preparation should also rehearse the couple for what it means to pray together as well as the meaning of the biblical readings chosen for the celebration. For his part, the presider should know that, at many weddings, he is speaking to many people who do not often come to the parish church. This is an opportunity to demonstrate our welcome and mercy.

ACCOMPANYING THE FIRST YEARS OF MARRIED LIFE [217–222]

217 Marriage is a matter of love, beyond physical attraction. Physical attraction wanes over time, but love never ceases. This requires a sufficiently long engagement period, one in which the couple grows together in love. If the preparation was inadequate, then the newly married couple needs to continue to grow.

218 Marriage is a lifelong process; weddings come and go quickly. Couples need to realize that they marry each other over and over again throughout life. Neither spouse can expect the other to be perfect; after the wedding, spouses should not expect to change each other into someone else, because this creates a marriage full of criticism, disappointment, and sadness. If they cooperate with it, the grace for this journey makes them generous, patient, tolerant, and full of love for each other.

219 "Young love needs to keep dancing towards the future with immense hope." If not, the marriage will grow stagnant because the couple will not learn to look beyond the arguments, conflicts, and problems that occur for everyone. **220]** Once a couple realizes with full force that they have given their life to each other with permanence and fidelity, the pleasure of belonging to each other sets in. The couple learns to negotiate differences without winners or losers. Both are winners because love is the force that drives this.

221 Unduly high expectations about sex can destroy a marriage. The excitement of the first kiss can dissolve into the reality that not all of life is that exciting. The solution, then, is not to think of separating but to enter into the process of growth that leads to deep happiness. The great mission of the couple is to help each other become more fully who they really are, forming each other for life.

222 We want to encourage the couple to be generous in accepting the gift of children. In this regard, "family planning fittingly takes place as the result a consensual dialogue between the spouses, respect for times and consideration of the dignity of the partner." The couple must form their consciences where they are alone with God, whose voice echoes in their depths. The pastoral leader accompanies the couple on this journey, helping them to reach decisions in accord with their consciences. "The parents themselves and no one else should ultimately make this judgment in the sight of God."

SOME RESOURCES [223–230]

223 Pastoral accompaniment needs to continue after the wedding. Experienced married couples have a strong role to play here. The newly married should be coached into the Christian way of life, prayer, and community.

224 Love needs time and space to grow. Time is needed to talk things over, reflect on them in light of what it means to die to oneself, gaze into each other's eyes, embrace leisurely, and appreciate one another's friendship. Pastoral ministry should not replace this but find ways to support and enhance it in the life of the couple, even in the midst of a fast-paced modern life. **225**] Couples must learn to spend time together, especially after the novelty of marriage has worn off.

226 Young couples should be coached to build into their marriage signs and actions of love: a morning kiss, a long chat over the first coffee, an evening blessing in bed, small gifts, trips, and shared household chores. Very important in this are celebrations together of birthdays and anniversaries; they provide the cadence of love. **227**] Pastoral ministry can also help them grow in faith as young couples. Teach them to speak with God as with a friend, sharing troubles and experiencing God's joy in their love.

228 Even when one partner is not Christian, common values can be found, raised up, and celebrated. All humans have an inborn hunger to be close to God. **229**] Parish leaders and the parish office should stand ready to help when called. Various movements, groups, and ministers should be prepared to do this. **230**] If the couple is not active in the local parish, be ready to welcome them when they do return. Baptisms, first communions, funerals, and weddings are opportunities to demonstrate how much we love them. Our pastoral care for these couples must reach out to them without smothering them in guilt or shame.

DISCUSSION

*In your own words, how do you describe what it means to "accompany"
someone on a journey such as in the first years of marriage?*

What ideas do you have for how that could become a reality in your parish?

*Who would do this: how, when, and with whose authority?
What would be most difficult about it?*

CASTING LIGHT ON CRISES, WORRIES AND DIFFICULTIES [231]

231 For those "whose love, like a fine wine, has come into its own," we offer congratulations and affirmation. "Old lovers," St John of the Cross said, "are tried and true." The sweet taste of love that has endured teaches us all.

THE CHALLENGE OF CRISES [232–238]

232 Family life always includes its own various crises. Facing and overcoming such moments creates an ever stronger love. Each crisis teaches us something important and allows the "wine of their relationship [to] age and improve." **233**] When a crisis is not faced squarely, it can erode the relationship. Communication is essential at these times!

234 The couple needs to work closely together to face whatever obstacle is in their path. They must learn to speak heart to heart and share their deep, inmost thoughts. I note that our research tells us most couples in these moments do not turn to the parish because they do not find it helpful; this teaches us that we have more work to do as a Church!

235 Some crises occur in almost every marriage. A crisis is a turning point, so this may include a pregnancy, a birth, and eventually an empty nest. **236**] Or the crisis may be financial, workplace problems, emotional needs not being met, difficulties with friends or family, or other disruptive moments. It may be a conflict or disagreement between the partners in the marriage; it may even have gotten to experiences of rejection, recrimination, or meanness between them. Learning forgiveness and the art of reconciliation, sometimes with outside help, is the pathway back to love.

237 Many people today believe that, when one or both partners feel unfulfilled for whatever reason—wounded pride, disappointment in love, jealousy, attractions to others, and so forth—sufficient grounds to end the marriage exist. If this were valid, no marriage would last! **238**] This is precisely the moment when the couple must rely on their commitment. Rather than thinking of themselves as martyrs, couples with mature love see the challenge as temporary and resolvable. In this way, throughout their marriage, difficulties arise and fade while love lasts forever.

OLD WOUNDS [239–240]

239 Some people remain emotionally immature well into midlife due to scars from previous hurts or unhappiness during youth. **240**] Many young people grow up without experiencing unconditional love from anyone. In most cases, this must be worked out in the context of the marriage, and the danger is that such old wounds can sabotage the couple. Outside help is sometimes needed, but an understanding spouse who listens carefully and responds with sincere affirmation is very healing.

ACCOMPANIMENT AFTER BREAKDOWN AND DIVORCE [241–246]

241 In some cases, divorce or separation—even though always the last resort—is the best moral choice a spouse can make for the sake of the children, or for his or her own safety. **242**] Pastoral accompaniment must show great tenderness and respect for people in these situations, which, sadly, are not uncommon. Efforts to reconcile should be attempted, and for those who are separated or divorced but not remarried, the Eucharist is a balm for the soul. For the poor, such family breakdown is even more painful since they have so few resources on hand to start a new life.

243 "[T]he divorced who have entered a new union should be made to feel part of the Church." They are not excommunicated. They belong to us because they continue to belong to Christ. There should be no discrimination of any kind against them. **244**] I have recently issued two important documents to simplify the process for declarations of matrimonial nullity (annulments). We want to reduce the time needed for this process and, if possible, the cost. Our concern is to guide people in these situations to understand what happened and repent for their part in it, if any, and to help them grow. This should happen at the local, diocesan level.

245 The children in a marital breakdown suffer the most! Parents, I appeal to you, never take your children hostage. Don't put the burden of your separation on them. Speak well of your former spouse whenever you are in front of your children. **246**] In general, we may often ignore the plight of children in situations where the family has dissolved. The pain they bear may last their entire lifetime. So pastoral ministers must not abandon or judge such children or make them feel less accepted than their peers.

DISCUSSION

How can your parish and pastoral leaders in your specific situation best accompany people during marital breakdown and divorce?

What attitudes must be present for this to succeed?

What happens to people now who are in that situation in your parish? How are they shown our love and mercy?

48

CERTAIN COMPLEX SITUATIONS [247–252]

247 Marriages between Catholics and other Christians can make a contribution to the ecumenical dialogue we desire. We should include the non-Catholic ministers in the wedding, and welcome and invite the non-Catholic spouse to take part in the life of the parish.

248 Likewise, marriages between Catholics and non-Christians represent an opportunity for interreligious dialogue in everyday life. We want to support such couples and help them integrate fully into the life of the parish. **249**] Baptism for people in complex marital situations requires the discernment of the local bishop.

250 We in the Church must imitate and reflect Jesus, "who offers his boundless love to each person without exception." People of same-sex attraction should be respected and treated with love. Any form of discrimination against them must be eliminated. We want to accompany these people to help them know God's will for their lives. **251**] Same-sex unions are not on the same level as marriage. **252**] Single parents, too, need our support and respect.

DISCUSSION

In what ways do we need to support couples
in these irregular situations in life?

What stands in our way or what enables us to do this?

What has been your own personal experience with this?

WHEN DEATH MAKES US FEEL ITS STING [253–258]

253 Death occurs for everyone, and our ministry to the grieving has long been part of our mission. **254**] Our outreach to families during the period leading up to death or following it must transcend all other boundaries. The Christian community responds, no matter what the situation of the family. **255**] Times of death are also times to question the meaning of life, the purposes of God, or even faith itself. At death, after a suitable period of grief, we must let go of our beloved ones and move on. And yet, they always remain with us.

256 Indeed, our faith teaches us that the dead remain in the heart of God and in the heart of our community. **257**] We pray in solidarity with our deceased loved ones, continuing the bonds of love that we held with them during their lives. **258**] The patterns of our life are the patterns we take with us into death. We can prepare for death by living in faith. "The more we are able to mature and develop in this world, the more gifts will we be able to bring to the heavenly banquet."

DISCUSSION

How does your parish support widows and others who have lost loved ones?

What has been your own personal experience with this?

CHAPTER SEVEN
Towards a Better Education of Children

259 "[F]or better or for worse," parents are the real teachers of their children. I want to discuss the role of families in detail.

WHERE ARE OUR CHILDREN? [260–262]

260 The household is the place where children are formed, and parents need, therefore, to be fully conscious about what their children are being exposed to via media, friends, entertainment, school, or the streets. **261** This does not mean parents should control every move of every child. If parents are obsessed with their children's whereabouts, it may drive the children away from honest dialogue. What is needed is for parents and children to talk together about "convictions, goals, desires, and dreams."

262 Prudence, good judgments, kindness, and goodness are not inborn; we must cultivate them and grow as persons. Parents help to form their children to understand their own lives and freely grow to adulthood.

THE ETHICAL FORMATION OF CHILDREN [263–267]

263 Moral formation for children remains the work of the parents. In this, their example is paramount. Children learn by seeing what their parents do. If children do not feel important to their parents, the result will be a damaged child. **264**] Parents can lecture their children all day long, but in the end, dialogue and example are the best teachers. Children must be helped to "learn for themselves" the values, principles, and norms of the Christian life.

265 "A good ethical education includes showing a person that it is in his own interest to do what is right." It is less effective to demand something than to point out how following the path of virtue yields benefits for life. **266**] Parents should coach their children to say "Please," "Thank you," and "Sorry." Repeating specific actions produces the building blocks of moral character. **267**] We free a child when we form him or her through example, experience, encouragement, and love. The child becomes free to love by our actions.

THE VALUE OF CORRECTION AS AN INCENTIVE [268–270]

268 We must also teach our children that misbehaving has consequences. Children should be coached to ask for forgiveness when appropriate, to make amends when they have wronged another, and to grow up as a vital part of the family.

269 Loving correction helps a child feel cared for. Parents don't have to be perfect themselves to do this, but children learn from their parents how to handle anger and how to judge right from wrong and when a mistake is just a mistake due to limitations or an extenuating circumstance. **270**] "It is important that discipline not lead to discouragement…" Parents must balance the need to discipline and affirm their child with helping their child realize his or her place in the whole family circle.

PATIENT REALISM [271–273]

271 We should not demand too much of a child, because this leads to discouragement. **272**] As children grow older, they can be helped to see how imperfections— which everyone has—are part and parcel of life. This helps them overlook such flaws in themselves and others. **273**] Psychology and educational professionals help us understand better today the difference between "voluntary" and "free" acts. A person may want to choose what is good but is unable to do so, due to upbringing or conditioning.

FAMILY LIFE AS AN EDUCATIONAL SETTING [274–279]

274 "The family is the first school of human values, where we learn the wise use of freedom." Children learn through osmosis—whether from parents or the media—and the lessons learned in the home last a lifetime. **275**] One of the chief lessons parents teach their children is to defer gratification. In the age of instant media, this may be a hard-learned lesson. Simply put, some things have to be waited for. One cannot have it all now, immediately, in this very instant. Learning to postpone some things until the right moment teaches self-mastery, which is a lesson that will be needed throughout life.

276 Children must also learn that the world and society are also our home. We live with others, and learning to socialize properly is important. It requires patience, listening, sharing, and respect. We learn all this in the family setting. **277**] The family is also the school in which children learn to consume a reasonable amount, throw away less, care for the environment more, and live on the earth as our common home. Likewise, the family is where children learn to cope during times of trouble, whether due to illness, loss, or natural disaster.

278 The media can help parents, but it may also hinder them. Parents must learn to use it wisely as a teaching tool. Such media cannot replace parents as the teachers, or the home as the place of love. Rather than sitting around the table with everyone on his or her own mobile device, create times of conversation and play that involve each other. **279**] Parents should be careful not to overly dominate their children. Children are raised by a community of people, each offering a dimension, all under the watchful eye of mom and dad. This includes the community of the school, the parish, family friends, and others.

DISCUSSION

What are the challenges we face in educating children?

In what ways does your parish reach out to coach young parents to become the first educators of their own children?

THE NEED FOR SEX EDUCATION [280–286]

280 It is not easy to approach sex education in an age when sexuality is as trivialized and commercialized as it is today. We need, however, a pedagogy of love and self-giving, and it is in this context that sex education makes sense. **281]** The information about sex that is passed on to children should be age-appropriate to help them develop a critical sense of right and wrong. With all the pornography, advertising, and other sexual stimuli present today, such discernment of moral values is more needed than ever.

282 A healthy sense of modesty is needed, allowing for privacy. **283]** It isn't enough to simply talk about "protection" in sex education as though everything can be reduced to what happens with our genitalia. Much more is needed! We are not mere objects to be used, either our own bodies or those of others. We teach sensitivity to various ways of expressing love, and we help them see sexual union in marriage as a sign of a lifelong bond.

284 Young people can easily be deceived into misunderstanding the role of sexual activity in their lives. "But who speaks of these things today? Who is capable of taking young people seriously? Who helps them to prepare seriously for a great and generous love? Where sex education is concerned, much is at stake." **285]** Sex education should help young people understand the differences between the genders and also to understand how God created us with the gift of sex.

286 Gender identity is the result of many factors, but masculinity and femininity are not rigid categories. When a husband takes on domestic chores or aspects of raising the children, he is not less masculine. When a wife takes on leadership and is the primary worker, she is not less feminine. Children should be taught to appreciate such exchanges as a healthy part of married life.

PASSING ON THE FAITH [287–290]

287 In today's fast-paced world, attending to matters of faith often takes a back seat to work, school, and other schedules. Nonetheless, the home is the place where faith is passed on. The parish cannot replace this with a program. This presumes that parents are themselves steeped in the faith. By teaching simple practices to their children, parents give them the tools of faith that will last a lifetime.

288 Children need stories of faith, actions to show faith, and explanations about what we believe. If children see their parents praying, they will become persons of prayer. **289**] The whole family has the task of passing on the faith. When children grow up in families where warm and friendly dialogue leads to actions of faith, they learn to cope with the imperfections of the world and do as Jesus did when he showed mercy to all and ate with sinners. **290**] By being in solidarity with the poor, by living simply, and by considering how its daily choices help sustain a healthy environment, the family is the school of life. All of this shows how we live the corporal and spiritual works of mercy and allow our Christian faith to guide our daily lives.

CHAPTER EIGHT

Accompanying, Discerning and Integrating Weakness

291 Even though the Church holds up the ideal of marriage as a permanent state that does not break down, we also hear the call to accompany everyone, including those who suffer through the loss of love in their lives and the pain of divorce. **292]** And for those who have remarried, we recognize that there are constructive elements in such unions, even though not living up to the ideal of Christian marriage.

GRADUALNESS IN PASTORAL CARE [293–295]

293 For those living in civil marriages or even in cohabitation, we note that the stability and care present there, the deep affection and shared responsibility for children, are also in need of our pastoral care with an eye to the eventual celebration of the sacrament. Even those who presently distrust marriage or put it off in favor of other values deserve our mercy and care.

294 The decision to cohabitate or live in a civil marriage is not always an outright rejection of the sacrament. It may be a rejection of "everything institutional" and often leads to a request for the sacrament. In some cultures, the sort of wedding expected of a couple is simply too expensive. All of these couples need to be welcomed and guided patiently. **295**] We know that we sometimes come to knowledge of moral goods by stages, gradually. This "law of gradualness" leads us to be merciful.

THE DISCERNMENT OF "IRREGULAR" SITUATIONS [296–300]

296 The way of the Church is not to condemn anyone, but to walk with them with mercy and reinstate them when ready. We must avoid judgments that do not always take into account the mitigating circumstances in which people live. **297**] Therefore, we reach out to everyone to help them find their own pathway of grace and take part in the local parish. This is true for the divorced and remarried, but also for everyone in an irregular situation. The Holy Spirit is working in the lives of these people, and our task is to assist in that.

298 The divorced and remarried, for example, are not a single class of people but live in a variety of differing circumstances. There may have been a brief first marriage, followed by a long second marriage in which children were received generously and raised in the faith; or there may have been a situation in which someone was abandoned, had an unfaithful spouse, or where every effort was made to save the first marriage, and so forth. The parish priest must discern carefully each situation, and no two are alike. There are no "easy fixes."

299 We want to more fully integrate those in irregular situations into the life of the Church, always avoiding scandal. They are baptized, after all; they are brothers and sisters. We want them to participate in every possible way, which requires "discerning which of the various forms of exclusion currently practiced in the liturgical, pastoral, educational and institutional framework, can be surmounted." They should not feel as though they are excommunicated but as though we value and love them.

300 Given the immense variety of situations we have mentioned here, it is clear that no new set of rules that would apply to all cases is possible. What is possible is to direct the pastors of the Church to undertake discernment of each case, recognizing that the degree of responsibility is not the same in all cases and, therefore, the rules may be applied differently from one case to the next. This is also the case regarding the sacraments and who is allowed to receive them, since in a particular case, no grave fault may exist. In this case, what I taught in *Evangelii Gaudium* 44 and 47 applies. Priests must accompany these people to help them understand their situation and be clear in their conscience, and this accompaniment must flow from humility, discretion, and love for the Church. We should never appear to have a double standard, and the burden for this falls on the pastors of the Church.

MITIGATING FACTORS IN PASTORAL DISCERNMENT [301–303]

301 The Church has a solid body of reflection that helps us understand how mitigating circumstances teach us that we can no longer say, simply, that any person in an irregular situation is in a state of mortal sin or is deprived of sanctifying grace.

302 The *Catechism* mentions such mitigating factors in article 1735. They include ignorance of the law, duress, fear, habit, and other psychological or social factors. There may be immaturity, acquired habit, or anxiety that lessen or remove any moral fault. "Therefore, while upholding a general rule, it is necessary to recognize that responsibility with respect to certain actions or decisions is not the same in all cases. Pastoral discernment, while taking into account a person's properly formed conscience, must take responsibility for these situations."

303 We also teach that individual conscience must be better incorporated into the practice of the Church in situations that don't embody our understanding of marriage. Conscience can recognize with sincerity and honesty what is the most generous and faithful response a person can make, given the circumstances, even if it does not correspond objectively to the rules. A person can come to see that a particular decision is in line with "what God himself is asking amid the concrete complexity of one's limits, while yet not fully the objective ideal."

DISCUSSION

How has your conscience guided you over the years of your life?

In your own experience or that of people close to you, share stories of times when what Pope Francis is teaching in article 303 came to light.

RULES AND DISCERNMENT [304–306]

304 "It is true that general rules set forth a good which can never be disregarded or neglected, but in their formulation they cannot provide absolutely for all particular situations." Nor can we ever argue that a discernment in one situation can then rise to the level of a general rule.

305 For this reason, no pastor should ever believe that it is enough to simply apply a moral law to people in irregular situations without regard to conscience, as though throwing stones at people's lives. This shows the closed heart of one hiding behind Church teachings. We must also see natural law as a source of inspiration for people making deeply personal decisions rather than as absolute norms. Likewise, it is important to note here that even a person who appears to be in a state we might consider objectively sinful may be at the same time living in and cooperating with grace and charity. Discernment is needed to learn how to best respond to God, and in certain cases, this may include the help of the sacraments.

306 In every situation where we address people in irregular marriages, we must clearly follow the way of charity. This is, after all, the first law of Christians.

THE LOGIC OF PASTORAL MERCY [307–312]

307 Just to avoid any possible misunderstanding, let me point out that the Church should never stop proposing the full ideal of marriage. When we teach the young, that ideal is what we teach them. By offering mercy to those in irregular situations we do not, thereby, change the ideal.

308 But we must also argue that, given our awareness of mitigating circumstances—psychological, historical, or even biological—without departing from the ideal, we can open our hearts and doors with mercy as people gradually make their way to holiness. I do understand that some pastors prefer a more rigorous application of the law that leaves no room for confusion, but I sincerely believe that Jesus is leading the Church to be like our mother who, while holding the ideal before us, also touches us with mercy and always reaches for what good is possible, "even … if her shoes get soiled by the mud of the street." Whenever we enter into the reality of people's real lives and know the power of tenderness, our own lives become wonderfully complicated!

309 We are considering all this by God's grace during our Jubilee Year of Mercy. In this year, we are following the behavior of Jesus, who goes out to everyone without exception. He loves us all, saint and sinner alike. **310**] We are called to show this kind of mercy because it has been shown to us. How dare we withhold it from those most in need of it? All of our pastoral ministry must be caught up in the tenderness of God's heart. I remind you again that the Church is not a tollhouse; it is the house of God.

311 The teaching of moral theology should include these considerations. We must always be careful to announce the ideal, but we must also always respond to people with God's free offer of love. At times we put so many conditions on mercy that no one can experience it; it is empty of meaning. This waters down the gospel and reduces it to a set of rules, cold and impersonal.

312 This resists that cold bureaucratic morality and replaces it with merciful love. I encourage all in irregular situations to speak confidently with their pastors to better follow the light of Christ. And I encourage the pastors to listen with sensitivity and a desire to help them live better lives in whatever circumstances they find themselves.

DISCUSSION

What elements of the pope's teaching here touch your heart most directly?

What challenges you in this teaching?

What affirms the decisions and pathways of your life?

CHAPTER NINE

The Spirituality of Marriage and the Family

313 There is a special spirituality that flows from marriage and family life, and I want to take the time to consider it here.

A SPIRITUALITY OF SUPERNATURAL COMMUNION [314–316]

314 God dwells in the hearts of those who live in grace, and the Trinity is present in the communion of marriage and the family. **315**] The Lord is present in families—in their daily lives filled with troubles and struggles and with joys and hopes. **316**] Experiencing family life is a pathway to holiness. Such a life helps us grow toward God. People in the midst of family life should not feel their family detracts from their spirituality.

GATHERED IN PRAYER IN THE LIGHT OF EASTER [317–318]

317 When a family is centered on Christ, his grace leads them through life. Moments of pain take you to the cross, and moments of exalted happiness to the resurrection. **318**] A few moments of daily prayer in the household can do wonders for the life of the family living there. Meal prayers, morning and evening prayer—all lead to deeper spirituality. But the Eucharist is the privileged place where the family's journey is renewed and strengthened.

A SPIRITUALITY OF EXCLUSIVE AND FREE LOVE [319–320]

319 Marriage is also the experience of belonging to another person. Spouses love each other and grow old together, and in this they reflect the face of God. So every morning we reaffirm before God our decision to love; every evening, likewise, we place our trust in God's leading hand.

320 The spiritual journey of each spouse, while joined, is also separate. Only God truly sees into the depths of each one's heart. By trusting in this, the couple lets go of unrealistic expectations and walks alongside each other, as God walks beside us each day. We learn that we do not so much belong to each other as to God alone. A great freedom results.

A SPIRITUALITY OF CARE, CONSOLATION AND INCENTIVE [321–325]

321 Let us care for one another as spouses with tenderness and mercy. Let us share in God's work and proclaim by our own lovemaking how much God loves us. **322**] We accompany one another through life with mercy. We leave a distinct mark of love on each other, drawing each other into the heart of God. **323**] What a profound experience to see our spouses and families with the eyes of God. We overlook no one; we embrace all; and we pay attention to one another's needs. What a tender experience of God this is!

324 The openness to life that is part and parcel of family life is expressed also in hospitality, welcoming and reaching out to neighbors, friends, and even strangers. Thus the family is both a domestic church and the way in which the world is transformed.

325 No family is perfect, but each is growing toward ever-greater holiness in Christ. We should not demand perfection from each other, should not judge each other harshly, but strive toward something greater than ourselves, something that is a gift to us, something we have been promised. May we never lose heart because we are frail, or ever stop seeking closer communion with God, who holds us tenderly.

DISCUSSION

In your own words, summarize what a spirituality of marriage is.

*How does family life reflect or fail to reflect the
face of God for you personally?*

PRAYER *to the* HOLY FAMILY

Jesus, Mary, and Joseph,
in you we contemplate
the splendor of true love;
to you we turn with trust.

Holy Family of Nazareth,
grant that our families too
may be places of communion and prayer,
authentic schools of the Gospel
and small domestic churches.

Holy Family of Nazareth,
may families never again experience
violence, rejection, and division;
may all who have been hurt or scandalized
find ready comfort and healing.

Holy Family of Nazareth,
make us once more mindful
of the sacredness and inviolability of the family,
and its beauty in God's plan.
Jesus, Mary, and Joseph,
graciously hear our prayer.
Amen.